Have you ever had to leave your body just to escape what's going on in front of you?

Imagine this happening almost every night for 6 years.

Let's step into a life machine and see life from my 6-year-old eyes. Prepare yourself things are almost NEVER what they seem and always viewed differently when you see things from down below

CHAPTER 1

“Everyone get your stuff on were going to Lola's house” - yells my mom from the other room

Paranoid and scared I stall and pretend to not find my shoes

“It’s been 15 mins pooh there's no way u can't find your shoes” - says my mom noticing I'm still not ready

“I'm coming mommy” - says my small voice as I realized I have no more time left to stall

Realizing that it's time to go to grandma's was always a love hate thing for me growing up. I come from a big family. My grandma Lola Howard had 15 kids and a big host of grandkids. It was always fun to think about being able to go see everyone and have a good time. But as we all know, with happiness there is dark trying to suck the happiness out and leave its cold cruel remains behind.

Before we get in too deep let's take a step back and break down the family tree. My mother Walttina Sykes was right smack in the middle of the whopping 15 kids. Now, as you can imagine, raising 15 kids was the mother lode of all loads right. Not for my grandma though she handled it with ease no one would have ever guessed such a small frail woman could have given life to that number of kids. Growing up 15 didn't seem like to much but now that I'm older and having my own kids 15 just seems insane! But she made it happen my dear old Lola! Growing up for my mom wasn't always the easiest I mean come on how would think your life would be growing up with 14 siblings and being right in the middle of all of them. As you can imagine, being a middle child in such a big family has its ups and downs but that's expected right? My mom wasn't always the easiest to deal with so of course her upbringing wasn't the easiest. Living between Hannibal Missouri, Qunicy Illinois and Davenport Iowa it was never enough with such a big family. She started her childhood in Missouri but that was short lived and moved to Davenport Iowa at just the small age of 4. Not Knowing the life trap set in front of her, the web created that would seem impossible to get out of.

Now my mom, despite all the obstacles placed in front of her, vowed at a very young age that this would not be it for her! Let's skip forward a few years to when me and my older sister come into the picture. My mom has 3 girls. My oldest sister Detisha, myself Calesha and my youngest sister Ariauna. Now Tish and I (that's what we called her) are only 4 years apart. Where Auna and I (Ariauna) are 8 years apart. So, when my mom was 16, she gave birth to my sister Detisha.

Exciting right, I mean yes, she was young but hey life gives you lemons you make lemonade right. She was my mom's pride and joy first child beautiful fun vibrant just a blessing to have. Of course, it was a new adventure and my mom quickly learned life wasn't so easy, but she would have another life to make a way for. She got to enjoy this for a nice long 4 years. As you can imagine, being so young things never really go as planned or how we want them to go. The child gets bigger, love doesn't turn out to be what you thought it would be and reality sets in and you must put your big girl panties on and do what's best for you and your child. So of course, she meets my dad, Cavette Jackson. Things are so smooth she's finally happy again and things are on the up and up and SURPRISE here comes another little blessing. This time it's me (the greatest gift ever lol) May 10, 1992, Calesha comes into the picture. Pooh became my nickname because of my bright skin tone and chunkiness. As you can imagine, fairytale life comes back into play and things will be much better this time right. I mean she's 20 experienced more and understands this thing called love a little better. But nope things go about the same and she realizes she's better off with her and her kids alone. A single mom at the age of 20 with 2 kids of course her mom will be there to help her, I mean come on she's raised 15 kids like a walk in the park she can help with 2 kids with ease. Your parents are your first role models so of course her first instinct was mom “can help me”. Not even realizing the strain that was to come from having a mother's help. She of course moved in with my grandma with 2 young daughters and bit the bullet and raised us the best way she could with her mother's support. As I explained before my mom was in the middle of 15 kids so that was not long lived. Trying to raise your own kids and there are still plenty kids in a household wasn’t the easiest or ideal situation, so she quickly got things together to have her own place to properly raise her kids. With the help of her mom, she was able to work a job to support her kids and household. For as long as I can remember my grandmother would watch me and my sister whenever my mom needed her to. Work fun events or just to have that mental break that life throws at you quite often. So, grandma's house became a second home. A very familiar place, that was the only option we really had. Being so young and not able to make choices for myself I would just go with it and enjoy the family time and fun I could have at grandma's house. Little did I know fun for me had a different meaning than fun for other people.

Time to dig in deep and start this time machine and jump forward to when the nightmare turns into reality.

CHAPTER 2

Ring ring ring playing with my toys I can hear my mom's phone ringing

“Hey girl what's up” my mom says picking up the phone

“What you doing tonight let's go out” not sure who's on the other end I hear the loudness through the phone

“Idk girl I got my kids” replies my mom

“Bitch if you don’t take them to Lola, you know she will keep them” says the caller

“Yea you right let me call her” laughs my mom

Before I know it, my mom comes in mine and my sister Tisha’s room and collect somethings for me and my sister and tells us “You're going to Lola's get ready” excited we both get our shoes and gather a few select things our self, ready to see the big host of aunt's uncles and cousins that’s always at grandma's house . Now I was born in the 90s, so grandma's house was always the place to be. Run around, do what you want and not have a single person to answer to. Well except those older cousins who always thought they ran the world. But nonetheless the freedom was endless. Now don’t get me wrong it was fun and free, but Lola knew when to put her foot down and that was the last thing you ever wanted her to do. So, we all knew how to have fun but stay out of her way as well. As we get in the car my mind is racing ready for all the adventures and things that would go on at grandma's house. But only if I knew this time would be the time of all times.

Pulling up to my grandma's house you could see the fun from down the street. 2 bedroom house with a few of her kids plus all the grandkids everyone would drop off. You could hear the chaos down the block, but you couldn't wait to get there and be a part of it and have all the fun in the world. We finally made it there after what felt like forever. My sister and I barely gave the car enough time to stop before we were clicking our seat belts off to go in and have the time of our life. All the love and excited family running up to the car to greet you with hugs, hits, kisses and everything in between.

"Couple hours Lola I will be back in the morning "says my mom while barely making it in the door. Now here's my grandma tiny frail little lady sitting on her bed working a 10,000-piece puzzle looking over her glasses with a blank stare not responding with any words just looks at my mom as she quickly scurries out the door. Nervous from the looks she gave I just stand still tiny and speechless waiting for her to stop looking so I can run off with everyone else. Tish on the other hand runs over to my grandma gives her a big hug and says “oooohhh that’s a lot of pieces what are you working this time Lola”? Even though she was our grandma she still liked to be called Lola. I never really knew why but the looks she gave me I didn’t dare ask her why I couldn’t call her grandma. The excitement of seeing Tisha and the looks I would receive walking through the door you would've thought it was two different people but nope just one great old Lola.

Let's take a second to paint the picture of Lola for you. She was a tiny frail old woman. Never really said much, just sat in her bed working puzzles watching her favorite shows. “Walker Texas Ranger” “Planet of the Apes” older things that brought her comfort I assume. Lola had her picks when it came to her grandkids doesn’t seem like a logical thing to say but if you ever came across her it would all make more sense. You never would know if you were one of those picks but oh trust me you would know if you weren’t! She would do the same things most days puzzles tv cook clean. Looking back on things now I don’t ever remember seeing her sleep crazy I know it seemed fine when you’re a child barely understanding life though.

The presence of her “pick” running up took her scold off me long enough for me to run off with the kids and see what kind of trouble they were getting into that sounded so fun on the pull up to the house. Catching up with the kids and seeing what the fuss was all about was always a mystery, were we climbing a tree, walking the railroad tracks, or my favorite going the store to be a distraction while the bigger kids stole all the candy we could eat. Excited and ready for all the fun “hey yall” I yelled out. “Oh, shit yea pooh can do it “- yells out my uncle Chris. He was the baby if the bunch closer to me in age, so I was always excited to hang out with Uncle Chris.

“Do what what are we doing” I said back egger to know what I was about to do.

“You the best distraction in the store I can get all their shit when you go in there” he replied slapping another cousin's hand excited thinking about all the goodies he was about to get.

Laughing happily “yea I will go you gone get me some candy to” I said quickly

“Duh my ninja why wouldn’t I you know Uncle Chrissy got you “he said as he put his arm around my shoulder making it sound even better to my intrigued ears!

So, it was set I would be today's distraction while he got all the good for us all to enjoy later. Being so young I still had to ask for Lola’s permission before I could leave. Chris on the other hand did what he wanted, he was the baby and permission was the last thing he was waiting for. Realizing that I had to go back inside and face my grandma to see if I could go, made my stomach turn with nervousness. Knowing that if I didn't ask her at just the right time when she was in just the right mood, that would be her foot coming down on me and I didn't want that. But it was now or never so I knew I had to suck it up and just go ask I mean come on I wanted that candy I HAD to have that candy. I went into the house and yup as you guessed it my nerves got the best of me, I walked right past her room and into the bathroom instead. Trying to pump myself up I looked in the mirror "you can do this you can do this. The worst she can do is say no" I whispered loudly to myself trying to make it seem easier. "You got this pooh just go ask" I closed my eyes took a deep breath and walked to her room. Lolas room was never intended to be a room but a 2-bedroom house with so many kids she made the best of what she had. She turned her dining room into her bedroom which had a sheet covering the entry way she used as her door. Pushing the sheet back slowly not too quick or too rough because that would surely change her mood and I would get a for sure NO!!

"Lola, can I walk to the store with Chris" I asked nervously. Lola slowly looked up from her puzzle, eyes instantly burning through me. "Who said Chris can go to the store" she asked me quickly. *Was this a trick question? I don't want to give the wrong answer. I thought to myself.* I instantly felt my face get hot as I just looked at her thinking hard and fast before I responded so that I didn't say the wrong thing.

"Chris going to the store I want to go" yelled Tish loudly taking my attention from the cold stare to realizing she was still in the room sitting on the floor in front of my grandma watching tv.

"Yea he said he got some money and I wanted to walk with him" I said looking back and forth between Lola and Tish making sure to avoid direct eye contact with her.

"Chris aint got no damn money. CHRISSSSS" Lola yelled out

"huh" Chris calls out.

Shit he's about to get mad at me now I thought to myself

"Mommy you called me" Chris says pushing through the curtain

"What money you got to go to the damn store. Let me find out you going to that store to steal again" she snapped at him quickly

"Mommy I still got some food stamps that you gave me the other day" he lies quickly

Dang he's good. My thoughts answering before Lola could

“When did I give you stamps Chris. You better not been stealing from me again because I tare you a new asshole mother fucker” she quietly said while going back to working her puzzle.

“Mommy you did” he lied again

It fell silent as she finds the place for her next piece

“Pooh gone walk with me and we gone come right back” he slid in to break the silence

“I'm going to” Tish jumped up

“Come on then we are leaving right now” Chris laughed

“And right back Chris. Get me some orange slices and my pop” Lola said slightly looking up from her puzzle while still working it at the same time.

“ok” he said walking away

Me and Tish both run out behind him as Lola continues to work her puzzle.

CHAPTER 3

Walking to the store Chris went over the plan and what everyone was to do while at the store, now having to add Tish into his plans. Excited, we all laughed and skipped to the store. Once at the store we all did as we were supposed to while Chris got all the goods. You see he was slick, while we distracted whoever was working at the counter, he would put everything out the back door to go around and get once we left the store. We happily headed back home with all the stuff we had. Knowing we had to share with everyone at the house we took out the things we got for ourselves that we didn't really want to share. Once back at the house all the other kids waited excitedly on the sidewalk for us to come back with all the candy for everyone. Coming back to a house full of kids with all the goods we had, we knew everyone's mouth watered which made us feel like we were super stars. Once everyone seen all the candy, their faces were shocked we had as much candy as we had. Hands out just waiting for their piece of the pie. No matter how much candy Chris got he always had his "share candy" and his "sell candy". Chris may have been young, but he was always ready to make his own spending cash. Now that it was back in the 90s there were still paper food stamps and shopping at Chris' candy store versus the actual store you were bound to get more for your buck. None the less everyone got their share of the candy, and we sat around laughing and enjoying the different flavors of all the different candies. Lola's house was well known but everyone knew it was only her grandkids there, no one else. We all played, had fun and stayed to ourselves. Once everyone was getting low on their candy, we all decided to go play on the apple tree next door. We all knew that this was off limits and Mr. Smiley hated for us to be all over his tree ruining all his apples by knocking them down. But hey when you're a kid living life forbidden things are the most fun so if it was a no our mind instantly told us yes.

As we all head over to the tree, we imitate Mr. Smiley's voice and make fun of how he sounded *"get out my tree" "go home"* we all laughed. When you walked up to the forbidden apple tree it was fairly close to the sidewalk and there were two stairs leading to a long walkway to the actual house. Knowing that it would take Mr. Smiley forever to get to us we always took the risk of having a little fun in the tree until it was time to run. Most of the time Mr. Smiley would just yell from his window and we would laugh at him and still climb higher in the tree. On this day though we played and played and laughed loudly and nothing. No *get out of my tree* or *go home* coming from the window. Maybe he just wasn't home or finally just got tired of yelling and running after us for us to still just climb his tree. Not caring that there was no distraction, we enjoyed our time in the tree before having to head inside because the streetlights were coming on. Once inside everyone crowds around each other being as loud as can be enjoying each other's company like we always did. Little did I know my life was about to change and things were about to happen to me that even today after 31 years old I still can't get over it.

“let's go downstairs and play hide and seek” one of my cousins said. Ready for the challenge of thinking of all the best spots to hide, we all get up and run down to the basement. Every house my grandma had one of her kids would have a room down there. Uncle Jimmy I would later in life refer to him as the devil. Not caring that that was his room we headed to the basement all with the mindset we had the best hiding spot and wouldn’t be found. There were two sides to my grandma's basement. One side Jimmy room, the other side empty with a few heat exhaust pipes around. As we sit in a circle playing “bubble gum bubble gum in a dish” to determine who would be the seeker Jimmy walks over. “What yall bout to play I want to play” he says quietly. Jimmy pretty much stayed to himself always down in the basement or not home at all. He wasn’t much of a talker, so no one ever really paid him much attention. “Ok bro u can play we seeing who it right now” Chris says back happy to have another player to make the game more interesting. Only if we knew just how interesting things were about to get. Chris finally finishes and deems the seeker.

“Go over there and close your eyes and count to 20 so everybody can hide” Chris orders someone around

“And don't try to peek because that’s cheating and if you cheat you gone count again” Chris bossed out

“Ok everybody GO HIDE” Chris yelled excitedly.

Everyone ran in every direction trying to make sure they were in the best spot not to be found. If you’ve ever played hide and seek you never want to be found. Being found meant you were the seeker next, and nothing is worse than playing a fun game and not being a part of the fun part with everyone else. Being that I was so small I ran over by the heat exhaust and squeezed in between sure I wouldn’t be found I giggled and got down as low as I could so I wouldn’t be seen. Everyone was getting tight and snug into their hiding spot as the seeker counted loudly to let you know how much time you had left before they came to find you. *click* the lights go off. I get a little nervous but don’t say much because I don’t want to be found. The room falls silent as the lights go off. “READY OR NOT HERE I COME” calls out the seeker. They move around looking under everything, opening doors, drawers and anything someone could be inside of. Little snickering sounds came out from people watching from their hiding spots seeing that the seeker isn't finding anyone. If you played hide and seek with my family, they would be far from fare. Everyone would move spots running to already searched spots just to avoid being found. Thinking that I had the best spot I stayed quiet and still waiting for the lights to come back on to know that someone had been found and I was safe.

As I sat waiting, I heard footsteps come towards me. Closing my eyes, I prayed the seeker didn't see me and I would be safe from being the seeker in the next round. The steps got closer and stopped. I closed my eyes tighter thinking It would make me less noticeable. The steps stopped but I refused to open my eyes. I heard everyone laughing and still running around so I opened my eyes saying to myself *whew that was a close one I thought I was caught.* Once my eyes opened there was Jimmy standing over me just watching me. "Scoot over so I can hide with you this is a good spot" he said slyly. "Yea come on but be quiet they not gone find me over me" I laughed realizing it wasn't the seeker and I was still safe. Or so I thought. Jimmy chuckled and got between the heat ducts with me. "Here sit on my lap so we both can fit, and my legs won't be sticking out" he said knowing his intentions. "ok" I innocently say as I stand up to let him in and turn to sit on his lap. I sat for what seemed like forever. He rubbed my back breathing heavily. I could feel his breath right on the back of my neck and his penis getting aroused. *Wait, what is he doing? What is that poking my butt* I thought to myself as the light turned on. "Your it your it" I hear the other kids yell out with laughter. I jump up and run out to where everyone else is gathered. Feeling nervous and very uneasy the game was not fun anymore and I felt something was wrong. “Pooh where was you at, I forgot you was playing” Tish said to me as I sat blank with my mind was racing. Never getting a chance to respond, the next seeker began counting. Franticly everybody runs in every direction trying to find their next best hiding spot. I'm not sure how to feel, the room got empty so fast as I sat in my thoughts trying to process what just happened. At that point I understood hiding alone was not safe. I ran to a spot my other cousins were at “no pooh you gone get us caught move” pushing me away I had to try a different spot. I ran to another spot where I saw my cousins hiding “nope nope nope u be moving too much you gone get us caught” another cousin said as I try to hide with them. Pushed away from two spots I go over to the stairs and just sit there. As I get lost in my thoughts still trying to process, I feel a rub on my knee. Scared to look up I do anyway, and it was Jimmy. Terrified at what was coming next, I tensed up and pulled away from him. He puts his fingers to his lips and signals me to be quiet. My heart drops and my soul leaves as he unzips his pants.

CHAPTER 4

Thinking back, I never really had many “talks” with my mom not sex not periods not unhealthy touches not anything of the sort. Now don’t get me wrong the older I get and being a mom now I understand a bit more as to why certain things were done a certain way when it came to raising me. None the less my mom was a great mom to me and raised me to the best of her ability at that time! You never know who you can trust, and you never realize it’s the people you can't trust until you can no longer trust them. My mom would have never sent me somewhere that she didn’t think was safe for me. So, with that being said talks weren't really something back then that people were big on or made a big deal about.

As I sit on the stairs Jimmy stands up and unzips his pants. Standing over me with his aroused penis in one hand he leans towards me, and puts is other hand on my head and shoves himself into my mouth. I let out a muffled cry and gag. He leans his head back and lets out a soft sigh. Enjoying himself while choking me with his aroused penis in my mouth he forces and forces while holding my head still to keep himself comfortable. I close my eyes and pray for it to be over. I don't know how long it will take because I tried my best not to even think. I realize what's still going on when I feel something going into my mouth and the back of my throat. At 6 years old I am so confused as to what's going on. The lights come on again and he pulls his penis from my mouth and proceeds up the stairs as if nothing just happened. I sit mouth full of whatever he left of him behind and I just hold it in my mouth, I sit there scared confused not knowing what to do next. Finally, I heard the others coming up the stairs, so I just turned and spit. I look down my eyes full of tears and see a creamy substance falling out of my mouth. Scared of everyone coming, I wiped my mouth and just sat quietly. "Aww look at the little baby mad she couldn't hide with us" one of my cousins taunted as everyone walked past me pointing and laughing as I sat with tears rolling down my face. “Pooh, are you ok what's wrong” I heard a soft voice say. I look up full of disgust to see my Aunt Amber holding her hand out reaching for me. “I want to go home can you call my mom” I cry as I throw my arms around her shoulders. “Aww pooh Walt will be back in the morning come on she says with such love. She then picks me up and takes me upstairs as I cry to myself not knowing what to do. That night was a blur, I just wanted my mom to come and be my safety and comfort. I'm not sure if I left my body or was just numb to everything going on around me but not much else came from that night. Just silent cries until I was asleep, and my mom came the next morning. When I woke up and it was time to go home it was almost like a bad dream. *Did that really just happen, am I dreaming?* Sorting out if it was a dream or reality was kind of far down on my list, I was still stuck in WHAT JUST HAPPENED. I didn’t say much to anyone or explain to anyone what happened. I mean how could I, I wasn’t even sure *if* it even happened. Excited to go home I ran and hugged my mom and said goodbye to everyone and got ready to go back home. Looking around, nervous and confused, Jimmy was nowhere to be found. Must’ve gone back to his dunging.

The thoughts I had after this moment led me down a road that I never would imagine I would go down. Being lost in the mind is a hard place to be lost, especially when you don't understand life like you thought you did. who would have thought that such a fun-loving place would bring so much hurt and trauma to a child. *Did people know? Does he remember what he did? What was that? Was it pee?* So many thoughts running through my little mind. *But who do I tell was it even wrong? Maybe I'm over thinking it and it's not even as bad as I thought it was?* Being that this had just happened the night before it was a lot to process a lot to understand and then I didn't even know if it was something that I even needed to process or work through. Little did I know it was the beginning of 6 long years that would feel impossible to escape.

Some time went by, and we didn't go to grandmas for a while. We pretty much stayed at home, and I sat in my thoughts stuck in a place I just couldn't escape. Things soon got back to normal, and I learned to silence my thoughts, stop thinking what if and stop constantly reliving a moment I didn't care to be in. Life got enjoyable again and I was feeling better.

CHAPTER 5

"Mom, can I go outside and play" I jumped begging my mom to get out to the open world.

"Did you do your chores and clean your room" my mom said softly uninterested in my excitement

"Yes, and I picked my dirty clothes up to" Still excited I said

"Ok fine but not too far stay where I can see you" she giggled noticing how happy I was to get out and play.

Excited and running as fast as I could through the house, I darted out the front door!

The neighborhood I grew up in was dull, not very exciting, but of course I would make my own excitement. I mean come on I'm young everything is an adventure for me! On the corner close to my house, maybe a block away, there was a payphone. Sitting lonely just waiting to be used. I couldn't resist, I HAD to call someone but who? I didn't know phone numbers that well I knew my house number, but I couldn't call there then my mom would know I was about to do something I was not supposed to. I got it 911. I can call them hang up and they will never know it was me. I could see if that worked and run back home with not a trace to lead back to me. It was settled I was going to use that phone!

I pick up the phone to dial tone. 9-1-1 I nervously push the buttons. With in a split second "911 what is your emergency" says the operator. I slam the phone down as quick as I can and run as fast as I can back down the block to my house and sit on the porch. Heart racing out my chest I lean forward to see if anyone noticed what I had just done. "How would they know it was me" I laughed to myself. That was funny, I must do that again. As I sat for a few seconds looking to see if the police were coming or if my mom would come out knowing what I had done. Nothing happened, no mom, no police, just me and my little sneaky plan happy we got away with it, I sat out on the porch enjoying the weather when I remembered *the sucker man.* Now right next door sits a little blue house with its perfectly cut grass. The house always had a scent of peppermint coming from it and a chubby old man sitting on the porch. As my focus turns from sitting on the porch I look over and I see a line at his door. *Oh yeah, I'm going to get a sucker.* These suckers were never free but he knew the kids on the block loved them so he would sit on his porch with a wicker basket next to him with a ton of suckers. *"What do you have to do for this sucker young lady"* and you would have to raise your hand and smack his and BAM you get a sucker. The quickest, easiest way and the most fun because everybody tried to hit his hand the hardest. I don't think anyone ever had too much power behind that high five, but sucker man would shake his hand and say ohhhhh that was a good one you're getting strong. Getting good grades in school and having proof of it would always get you more suckers and that WAS the best prize. On this day once I seen all the kids lined up waiting for their sucker, I noticed a little girl with hair flowing down her back. She had to be a princess hair long beautifully flowing. I just had to see who she was and tell her how beautiful her hair was. Standing in line waiting for my turn to get my sucker I didn't take my eyes off this long flowing hair, just a few people in front of me. She gave sucker man a high five and turned around as her hair flew behind her and she turned around with the most angelic soft loving face. “Thank you” she smiled as she grabbed her sucker and continued her way down the street. I quickly gave my high five and ran off the porch to find this long flowing hair. She sat there just three houses down from mine on the stairs smiling and enjoying her sucker. Now I wasn’t the most talkative child but what the hey she's right here by the house we can say hello to each other that would be fine. I skipped down the street pretending to just walk to the corner so that I could walk past her. She gave a slight smile as I skipped past her. I went all the way to the corner and told myself ok on the way I will just tell her how pretty her hair is. “You have really pretty hair” I say as I skipped back past her. “Thank you, you want to come play with me” she said so happily as if she's known me for quite some time. “SURE” I said with a big smile. I walk over to her, and we go to her backyard.

“I'm Ruby” she says reaching her hand out to shake mine.

“I'm Calesha” I smile and shake her hand back.

From that moment on when I would go outside, I would go three houses down and knock on the door. “Is ruby home” I would ask. I didn’t have very many friends I would pretty much play by myself but now I had a friend around my age to explore and have new adventures with. “She will be right out” says her mom would say!

Ruby comes out and says “come on let's go in the backyard” I follow her lead and just go to the back. We climbed a couple trees, played tag and played a couple of hand games. After running all through the backyard laughing, playing and having the best time of our lives, Ruby’s mom yells from the porch. “Do you girls want a popsicle?” “Yes” we say at the same time and laugh loudly that we said it at the same time. We walk around to the front of the house and sit on the porch enjoying the cool popsicles while the sun shines down on us with a cool breeze.

“How long have you lived here” I break the silence

“Not that long this is my grandpas house me and my mom just moved here” she said still enjoying her popsicle

“I'm glad you moved here it be boring sitting outside all the time with no friends. I don’t get to go very far my mom said she has to be able to see me” I said rolling my eyes like that made me not cool or something

“Yea I can't go very far either, so I just sit on the porch or go in the backyard” she said not caring about the restrictions.

It got quiet again then she looked over and I looked back at her, and we both started laughing for no reason again. It was a good day. We finished our popsicles, and her mom eventually told her it's time to come inside and wash up for dinner, so I went home.

"Mom, I like my new friend'' I say running through the door "her hair is super long mom she got hair that go all the way to her feet" I said before she could even respond to the first thing I said

"that's nice what's her name is she nice to you" my mom said as she continued getting dinner ready for me and my sister.

I excitedly told my mom about my day and as she continued to finish what she was doing. I had finally had a day worth talking about that I didn't have to feel so crappy about it, that was the best feeling for me. Life was finally starting to look good for me again. I was able to push things to the back of my mind and not think abut I as much anymore.

CHAPTER 6

I'm not sure the reason but we didn’t go to my grandma’s house too much for a while and when we did my mom was there and he was not, and we didn't stay to long. This was great for me. I wasn’t to concerned about the space we were having. Yes, I missed my cousin's aunts and uncles (a select few but it was better for me this way anyway.) I went on with my young life but became distant and more aware of certain things. Of course, the space didn’t last long and the trips to grandmas became more frequent and I was eventually left alone without my mom. My plan was to just always stay with someone I avoided ever being alone because I knew if I was by myself that it was easier to be a target.

One day it was cold and raining hard. My grandma had a full house. Everyone had dropped their kids off and there just wasn't much to do because of the weather.

"Everybody go upstairs I'm about to put a movie on" my grandma said to everyone as we sat there bored, being loud because we had nothing else to do. Heading up the stairs something felt very off to me call it intuition or whatever you want to call it, but it just wasn't right. The room was not very big as you might imagine so we were all lying close together. Covers were spread out on the floor, and everyone just had to find a spot to fit and lay down. I snuggled next to my aunt Amber, that was the safest choice, or so I thought. Laughter and jokes filled the room as the movie went along and funny things happened. *Cool I can relax I'm ok* I thought to myself. But I guess I spoke too soon the movie was coming close to an end and most of my cousins were either asleep or falling asleep. I see the door crack open and eyes peer in. Jimmy's face comes into the light and my heart sinks once again. My body shuts down and I feel the tears choking up in my throat. I scoot closer to Amber and put my arm around her realizing that she was asleep too, I just closed my eyes and prayed that he just turned around and left the room and didn't bother me. But I was wrong yet again he looked around the room as if to see what he could get away with. He looks at me and I try my hardest to beg with my eyes *please no just leave* I thought to myself as he walked over to me and got in the cover behind me. I try to scoot even closer to Amber, maybe he will leave me alone if I'm too close to her! He grabbed me around my waist and pulled me closer to him. I tense my body hoping he feels the fear in my body language, but he doesn't care he only thought about himself. He rolls me slightly on my side and pulls my legs apart slowly forcing his rough hands all on my thighs. I try my hardest to pull away from him, but it doesn't work. He whispers so quiet but strongly "open up" I let out a whimper hoping that he can hear how uncomfortable he is making me, but he still doesn't care. He decides to force his fingers into my tiny hole. Not caring how bad it hurts me, not caring that this is a sacred space, My sacred space and not for him! I close my eyes and imagine being somewhere else. I can't tell you how long this went on because the next thing I remember is waking up and everyone was being loud, playing, jumping and running around. That was the first time that I completely left and never came back mentally. There were so many times that I wished I could leave and never come back physically. But I could only escape mentally, that would be the best escape ever though just leave and be in whatever great place I could make it to be.

Not much changed as the years went by I just became more and more numb . Blocked more of life out than I ever thought I would have to, there was no escape and I just had to deal with it is how I felt. Was that true was there really no way out was I stuck in this forever. By this point I'm almost 8 and this was pretty much my normal life. I had no outlet, I became angry. Acting out in school getting into fights talking back to teachers stealing from my mom everything that would help me let the anger out well I thought was helping me let the anger out . At this point in my life I started hanging with my cousin Megan. Now she was my favorite, she was a spoiled brat all she ever did was cry suck her thumb and get her way and I loved it. She was easy to get along with because if she was getting what she wanted that meant I was getting what I wanted . Where can I go wrong with a plan like that right. Now her mom Kristen was a sweetheart she let me come over as much as I wanted, she let me go run errands with her, help he with things around the house, just accepted me with open arms and I loved it. We all know that great things come to an end at some point though. At this point so many things had happened to me that I had a horrible fear of basements. I honestly after all this time still have a fear of basements. It's a big trigger for me and I just cant handle the way being "down under" makes me feel. But at Kristen's I felt safe I would go down in her basement with her and help with her laundry, sort, fold, load the washer, change the clothes to the dryer the usual stuff, just being helpful to her . But there was something very familiar about her house I wasn't sure what it was but I just knew that uneasy feeling never really went away so my guards were always up. There was literally no way I was going to let something like that happen to me again. This was my escape I had finally got away from my nightmare I wasn't going back. But just like a cold night it always comes back around. Remember the crybaby spoiled brat I told you Megan was, yea she would lay in her room with me and when she thought I was asleep she would get up and go lay with aunt Kristen in her room. On this night though I couldn't sleep I tossed and turned for the longest and sleep was just not on my side. Just when I got comfortable and thought I would finally get some sleep, I see the light shine through a slight crack in the door my nightmare was back but this time with a different devil. The look in his eyes the feeling of uneasy all the same signs there laughing at me choking me making sure its presence was well known. Was I really about to go through the same nightmare with a new monster. I closed my eyes and just prayed "please don't let this be happening again" and before I knew it my next monster was right there right next to me rubbing touching exploring my body like he had the right. Once again such a safe place an escape from everything turned into the next place I needed to get away from. Now Derrick was different from Jimmy. He would get more physical he wanted to get every experience out of the situation he could. Laying there once again mentally gone and just waiting for things to be over as he rubbed my non existing breast. *What feeling could he possibly get out of this shit* I thought to myself *there's nothing there*. He continued to rub me and leaned in for a kiss, I didn't know what to do I just sat there blank my usual response. He forced his tongue in my mouth and shoved it all around. *"this is so gross is he spitting in my mouth"* I thought to myself. The more he kissed and rubbed all over my small body I noticed a bulge coming through his pants. I pulled back hoping he would know I was uncomfortable and leave me alone. Once again he didn't care, just like all my other encounters before, only thinking of them selves, not me, my mind, my feelings, he continued as he grabbed my hand and slowly put it in his pants. I pull my hand back as I realize where and what he's placing my hand on. He pulled harder and forced my hand up and down on him self. I ball my fist and close my eyes just waiting for it to all be over. I don't know if he got a sense that someone was awake or just that things weren't right because he forced me to stroke his penis a couple more strokes then got up and went back into his room. A few seconds later my aunt Kristen came out her room and went to the bathroom. As she walked back to her room she looked in the room as I lay across the floor just looking at the ceiling "pooh you still up girl " she giggled as she walked in her room and closed the door. I sat for hours just wondering, asking myself *what is wrong with me . Why do people keep doing this shit to me. Am I to pretty , do I do things that make them think I want this shit to happen, am I jus a fuck toy? WHAT IS GOING ON.* Hurt confused and just lost I close my eyes as tears roll down my face and I force myself to fall asleep. The next morning I woke up to my cousin Megan seeing if I was awake. "you want to go to the store wit me and mommy, she's bout to be leaving so you better come on". I jumped up and put my shoes on, there was no way I was about to stay in this house with no one there just me and "the monster". I was pretty quiet the car ride to the store didn't try to get anything just walked around blank lost in my thoughts. I don't remember much from that day I guess my thought must've been to over bearing. That night I wanted to go home but I thought to myself and said maybe he didn't mean to I will just try to stay again but make Megan stay in here with me. I'm not letting her go in Kristen room, and if she does I'm going with her I planned to myself. Now Megan as I mentioned was SPOILED ROTTEN. She had every single Mary Kate and Ashley movie you could think of and I LOVED to watch them all and sing the songs. So of course she pulled out her collection and the vcr player as we laughed and decided which one we would watch. After debating which one would be the best one to watch we picked "Mary Kate and Ashley sleepover". We had snacks popcorn the worlds best pallet and we were ready to get this movie night started. We laughed and sang so loud as we jumped around pretending we were at their slumber party instead of our own. As usual such a horrible night created such a beautiful day after. It was like nothing happened I could relax and not worry or think about it. We had to have watched 2 or 3 movies when Megan finally started giving signs that she was tired. We laughed and joked about her being a baby and that she was just waiting to get in her moms bed. She didn't care though she was proud to say she was scared and she was sleeping with "mommy" as she would say. Having so much fun and enjoying my night I didn't think to far into the conversation until I fell asleep and woke up to a hand sliding under me while I slept on the couch. "shh I'm going to put you in the bed" a voice said as he picked me up off of the couch. Still half asleep and wanting to fight the hand off of me I just let him pick me up. I felt the coolness of a pillow as I was laid down out of the arms of who ever just picked me up. I barely open my eyes to look over and see the light shining from the hallway noticing the bathroom as the door close . I start to close my eyes and I realize "THE BATHROOM". If I was looking at the bathroom outside of the door then that meant I was IN DERRICK'S ROOM! I tried to jump up as he grabbed me and said "its ok pooh everybody sleep you might as well lay down" once again I just had this feeling that I just KNEW I wasn't about to like what came next. I close my eyes and just wish to be somewhere else as he waste no time pulling my panties down. He slowly began licking me between my legs as I wonder *what is this feeling I'm feeling. I have to pee I don't know what's going on*. He continues for several minuets as he moans and makes noises while rubbing my chest . I close my eyes and wonder when its going to be over. The second I close my eyes he stops and slides his body on top of mine. The closer to the top he gets I can again feel his erect penis. Helping himself between my legs and starting to kiss all over me in places I didn't think people kissed you on. I lay silent just waiting for it to be over, for him to stop. He stops kissing me and looks me in my eyes as he is laying on top of me. I give the most pleading sorrow look as my mind could help me make. He doesn't break his eye contact just keeps looking me in my eyes as he grabs himself and tries to insert his erect penis inside me. I instantly start crying it hurt it burns it just does not feel very pleasant. He doesn't shove hard but he shoves persistently. As he continues to try and try but it does not go in he begins to roughly rub himself up and down making our genitals touch. I cry because the feeling is just not great. I jerk my body trying to pull away from him being on top of me. He stops looks me in my eyes again and lays on the side of me. I continue to lay on my back with my hands up waiting for the "ok" to get up. He doesn't say anything just starts pulling on himself and making noises. I lay silent just waiting for what was next. *"what do I do , can I get up why am I still sitting here"* he lets out a soft sigh of relief as his strokes slow down, stopping m thoughts and catching my attention. He releases him self in his hand and gets up and finds something to clean his self with. "Go in Tif room pooh" he says quietly as he pulls his boxers up and climbs back into his bed. I jump up with out even thinking twice and run to the bathroom .

CHAPTER 7

I stand still quiet in disbelief as I look at myself in the mirror. I finally zone back in and just look at my small angelic face. I just cry ball like never before. I look at my hands, my legs, my body, just everything. Is this really what my life is going to be? Am I just always going to have to do this for people? Why do I always have to be the one to do it? So many emotions going through my mind and body as I realize I feel a stinging sensation between my legs. I sit down to pee and jerk as it starts to burn while trying to go pee. I start to get worried. I don't know why it feels like this, and I become very scared. Afraid to wipe and look at what was happening down there. My small mind thought I was going to wipe and my entire vagina was going to be on the tissue, its funny now thinking back. (The whole thing coming off like come on girl). But again I was young my mind was not to a point of understanding the things that were going on in my life. I sat with the tissue pressed on the part that hurt and just prayed it was all ok. After a few seconds of holding the tissue there I pulled it off to look at it and saw a small amount of blood. My mind instantly went to the worst and I begin to cry harder not knowing what was happening or how bad the situation was I just sat in disbelief . *What do I do now do I need to go to a hospital am I going to die.* So many horrible scenarios going through my mind before I finally decided just wet a wash rag in cold water and sleep with it right there. Now that I'm older thinking back on the situation it was probably tares to my skin just from being so small and not ready for the things that happened. It was not a flowy flow of blood just spots on the tissue as I wiped but to me I was dying. I grabbed the rag ran cold water on it and slowly and gently sat it between my legs as I pulled my panties and pants up. I wanted to stay in that bathroom forever but I knew that just couldn’t happen. I wiped away my tears and prepared to walk back out into this horrible moment. I felt so safe in the bathroom I felt like no one could touch me it was just me, God and my thoughts . No interruptions no one coming in no one checking just me like I liked it . I finally open the door and the house is silent, everyone's door is closed and all I can hear is the sounds of fans and slumber. I walk to Megan's room and lay down. It hurt to walk, it hurt to move, so I just laid on my side with the cool rag and my hands between my legs. I almost instantly fell asleep must've just been so exhausted from crying and mind exhausted from being so confused. The next morning when I woke up I wasn't in as much pain. It didn't hurt to walk and I was just more comfortable than I was the night before. Oddly enough I never really seen Derrick that next day. I honestly didn't care I didn't want to see him. I was ready to go home but of course I had to wait until my aunt wanted to take me I just sat around most of the day didn't want to go outside and play, just wanted to sit on the couch and do nothing. Finally it was time for me to go home. Once I got home I just felt disgusted with my self. I wanted to understand I wanted things to make sense but they just didn't. I was about at a junior high age at this point so I was learning my body learning what certain parts were made for and things of that nature. I pretty much acted like nothing was wrong once I got around my mom and sister. "Hey" I said stalely as I walked in the house. "Hey pooh you have fun" my mom said. "umm humm" I say as I continued to walk to my room, knowing I just wanted to wash life off of me at that moment. I got all my stuff together as I prepared to take a bath . I needed to soak I needed to get this feeling off of me, I needed to get

HIM off of me his smell, his body, just all of it. I made my water extra hot as I stripped out of my clothes preparing to get in. Still disgusted with myself I couldn’t even face the mirror I kept my back turned as I became more and more bare in my reflection. How can I ever face myself again I can never look at me the same. I stepped into the tub slowly due to the water being so hot. Once fully in my body adjusted and it didn’t seem so hot anymore. I sink down into the tub as my vagina begins to burn again. I sigh as I begin to cry thinking about the things that just happened. I sob and sob and some more as I just continue to get lost in my thoughts again, seemed like a spot I just couldn't get away from lately. I cry for what felt like forever when I look over and see my moms razor sitting on the edge of the tub. I stop crying and pick it up as I turn it around over and over again looking at it wondering just how sharp it actually is. I realize my thoughts and hurry and put it down. I began to scrub my self clean as I try to get rid of the filth left on my body. By the time I get out the tub I can smell dinner is cooking so I go in my room and put my things away knowing I would have to go around my mom and sister and act like nothing is wrong. “Yall wash yall’s hands and come eat” yells my mom making sure her voice is heard upstairs for us to hear. I come down and sit at the table and not say much . I pick over my food but eat just enough for my mom not to yell at me for not eating. I finish as much as my stomach will allow me to and help my sister clean the kitchen. Chores were a big thing in my house and cleaning the kitchen after dinner was always a must that me and my sister had to do, I clean and get the kitchen together as quickly as I can so I can just go back to my room, just be alone just like I liked it. I hurry past everyone trying to make it to my room because I feel myself about to break as thoughts are starting to run through my mind again. “get your school clothes together and get the stuff so you can get your hair done” my mom yells as I think I'm getting by quick enough to not be noticed. Now I have to suck it up and be viewed how everyone views me "happy fun loving life pooh".

Going to school was sometimes fun and a great way to escape. I was very smart. I LOVED math and I loved to read. Reading was a great release I discovered and got pretty used to it. The week goes by, and I begin to forget just glide through and act as normal as I could act. The weekend rolls around and I miss my cousin. I wanted to go back and out with her, but I didn't want what came with hanging out with her. I sat in my thoughts trying to figure out if going to have fun with her was worth the trauma brought into my life. As I go over the pros and cons of going over to my cousin's house. I can hear my mom on the phone. "I don't really care, we can" she says as she is walking throughout the house. She talks a little more, giggles and hangs up the phone. "What are you doing mom" I say curious as I come down the stairs to see what's going on with her. " I think Ima go to hang out later" she smiled just thinking about all the stuff she was gone get into. *"I guess I might as well go"* I roll my eyes to myself as I walk back up the stairs. Hoping everything will be ok, I get stuff together to go to my cousin's house. Now yes, I asked my mom to go but being that it was her sister's house she didn't really care that much when I wanted to go over there.

My mom and her siblings were pretty close growing up as far as keeping us all together. Yes, we had a host of family members outside of my grandmother's kids, but they pretty much stayed between the 15 of them. We didn't really deal with other family members as much as we did with each other. Prepared to go over, I call my aunt's house phone to see if it's ok for me to come over. "Hello" said Megan as she answered the phone. "Hey Tif, can I come stay the night" I laughed thinking about all the fun we would have while I was there. "Yea I don't care" she laughed, excited I was coming over. "Ok I'm about to walk over" I say as I grab my bag. We were not very far from my aunt's house. There was a corn field behind my house that if I just ran across it, I was a couple houses away from my aunt's. Thinking back to those days Tish never really went to very many places, mostly just Lolas, she loved going over there. It never really crossed my mind to ever wonder if things were happening to her over there, I was just pretty much glad to not be over there. I grabbed my things and headed down the stairs to head to my aunt's house. "Mom, Kristen said it was ok if I come over, I was about to walk over there" I say walking past my mom sitting on the couch. "Ok love you let me know when you make it" she said as I walked out the door. On the walk over I tried my best not to think about the bad and just focus on all the fun we could have. I mean Tif had everything at her house, all the Barbies, all the toys, a stereo with good CDs. Everything a girl like me loved. I feel a smile going across my face as I think about seeing her sitting there sucking her thumb. Boy she loved that thumb. I put my thumb in my mouth to see how it felt. "Eww gross" I burst out laughing to myself realizing there was nothing special about it. Before I knew it, I made it to my aunt's house. Beautiful two-story family home. Light blue, just perfect. I always looked at her house and just smiled. It had the same address as my grandma's house, and it just always tickled me. Same numbers just different streets. *What were the odds* I would think to myself. walking into Kristen's house it was always something going on. Her kids and grandkids playing, crying, eating, just always noise. I loved the noise though; the silence was what I hated. Too much silence meant evil was lurking around, I would always say. I walk in and take my shoes off and head up the stairs. Now when you walk in there's a few stairs leading to the living room and a few stairs leading to the basement. I walk up and see everyone sitting around just enjoying each other's company. “Hey, pooh lovey” my aunt says as I walk in. “Hey Kristen” I said smiling. I loved being around Kristen, she just always made me feel so warm and loved. She had the most beautiful thick black hair. Sometimes when I came over, she would get her hair grease and let me grease her scalp and just play in her hair. I loved moments like that because her hair was always just so amazing to me. She smiled and looked back over at the tv. I joined everyone and just sat around trying to see what everyone was doing. A few minutes after being there Kristen gets up and heads down the stairs. Now I think Kristen LOVED doing laundry because it's like every time I looked up, she was in that basement switching loads and bringing loads up. Another few mins go by, and she comes up the stairs carrying a basket. She sets the basket down and begins to grab things out, folding them and setting them to the side. I sat on the couch across from her just watching, admiring how she would just glow and smile. Always so happy and content with her life.

She eventually looks up and smiles, noticing me watching her. “Wanna fold the wash rags pooh” she said softly as I smiled back. I nod my head and jump up eagerly to help her. Her laundry always smelt so good it was always so warm. Helping her fold the laundry really gave me relief. I was able to feel helpful and enjoy the warmness of the clothes. As we finished the basket, she was not paying attention to anything else, just the clothes in front of us. She turns on her music. Now Kristen’s choice of music was always the best, just so chill and so much meaning. When she would turn on her music I would always just laugh because I knew she was going to get into her cleaning mode and just move around so fast picking things up just singing her heart out. It was really the best feeling, just the feeling of enjoying life and watching other people enjoy it.

CHAPTER 8

As a child I found out at a young age that I loved seeing other people be happy. The joy of seeing them enjoy life just brought a lot of happiness to my heart. I wasn't really a bad kid in my opinion. I did get to a point where I was a lot to handle sometimes, but due to the trauma I'm surprised I wasn't worse. I was your typical pre teen I wanted to paint my nails, read, write and just enjoy friends. I had a lot of friends in school I went to Wood Intermediate, and it was full of trouble. All these different pre teens with all these different personalities it was a blast. I would talk to pretty much every one, I liked people who knew how to be a good person to me. I was really big on treating people how I wanted to be treated, I still am. So as long as you were nice to me I was nice to you. That weekend wasn't a horrible weekend. We played, had fun, laughed, sang and just acted like kids . *"I can get use to a normal weekend"* I think to myself as I was in the car on the way home . “Bye see you next weekend pooh” Kristen said pulling into the drive way of my house. “Bye love yall” I said jumping out the car to go in the house. Once inside I head straight up to my room. Happy and content that I was finally able to just have fun and nothing happen to me. “Pooh is that you, Get in the shower because I know you didn’t while you as gone” my mom yelled from her room. I cracked up laughing to myself as I sat on my bed as I thought to myself *“you show right I forgot all about that”*. I get my things together and get ready to take a shower. I head into the bathroom and turn the water on. I sat all my things on the toilet and notice a light reflecting in my side view. I look over and it’s the light reflecting off the mirror. “I’m not looking in that” I roll my eyes as I realize its nothing I thought it was. I sit for a second looking over at the mirror from the side. *“why not though?”* I think to myself. I take a step over and close my eyes as I get in alignment with the mirror. I take a deep breath and prepare to open my eyes. I open my eyes and just stare blank at my reflection. I touch my cheeks and my hair trying to process what I'm actually looking at. After a few moments I shake my head . “You are so damn ugly, what they seeing in you anyway” I say to myself as I quickly turn away from the mirror. I touch the shower water to test the temperature before I get in. I take my clothes off and step into the shower. Sitting there in the water my mind starts to race . *"What made this time different from the rest? Why didn't I see him, why didn't he mess with me?"* I thought to myself. Now some people may call me insane or think I'm just plain crazy. Who wants to be touched who would ask why someone isn't doing things to them that they don't want done? But that was not the case. No I didn't want to be touched and no I didn't enjoy being touched but there was something in me, in my mind that wondered why it didn't happen. Call it trauma call it what you want but my mind thought what it thought. As I begin to wash up cleaning off my weekend and the stink. I laugh to myself thinking about all the trouble we got into and just the comfort I felt from being around my aunt and cousin. Of course where there's good thoughts there's bad thoughts. I've learned in life this is duality. As much as you embrace your good you have to embrace your bad. Life is full of balance and until you take on your good and your bad your never going to understand your life fully. As the thoughts of the fun fade away I begin to remember the last time I was over there. I begin to feel disgusted, thinking of his body on mine, thinking of his tongue in my mouth. I fight back tears as I wash my arms trying to push the thoughts out of my head. Tears begin to fill my eyes before I know it. *"Why would you do that to your self, why would you even remember that when we want to forget"* I think to myself as I scrub harder. I finish washing up and began to rinse off as I try to crowd my mind with something else, anything else I just didn't want to relive that again. As I scramble trying to find something to think about I look over and see my moms razor on the shower caddy under the shower head. I take a step back and just look at it as it looks back at me. I reach over and pick it up as I wonder about its blades inside. I turn it around and look it over, mind racing to fast for me to catch the thoughts. I look it over to see if its even possible to come apart. I shake my head and put it back in the caddy as I turn the water off and get out. I dry myself off and look up to realize I'm back in front of the mirror. "Ugh" I say with disgust as I try to avoid fully looking. I walk out the bathroom and head over to my room. I put my clothes and things away and wonder what my sisters doing. I walk next door to her room and see her door is closed. Tish always had her door closed. Even though she was the oldest she was the biggest kid at heart. I loved that she didn't let her age define her. She was going to be Tish no matter what father time told her what time it was. "Come in" she yelled as I waited for her to hear my knock. I push her door open to see her barbies laid out. I crack a small smile as I ask "What you doing" . "Playing barbies, look at her room" she pointed. She was always so creative. She would use what ever she could find and make the best houses and things for her barbies. Vcr tapes, all the wash rags from the hall closet, socks you name it. She wanted to give them the lavish life I guess you could say. I look at the barbie room completely uninterested "that's cool how long it take you to do that" I asked just to have something to talk about. "not that long why you want to play" she asked. "Sure" I shrug my shoulders. I had no interest in barbies like her. She loved barbies, babies, and everything typical kids loved. Yes I know I talked a lot about Megan's barbies, babies, and toys but she always had the best new stuff . I didn't have to build the house's and find stuff to make the beds it always came with that type of stuff. The way Tish played her imagination was so big she could look at two pencils and a sock and make the best king size bed with a nice cover to go with it. I must've had to much on my mind because I could never look at things and see the vision like she could. If it wasn't already made in front of me I had no interest in making it! I sat on the floor with her as she handed me all type of barbies and supplies to make their house nice. She was so excited talking about "Girl Ima come over with my baby when you done with your house" I couldn't help myself but to laugh at her because she wasted no time getting into character for her barbie's and I was barely even in the mood. Seeing her excitement made me happy though so I did my best to act like I cared, and made the best I could make with the stuff she gave me. We laughed and played and we pretended our barbies were hanging out. Before I knew it my mom was calling out "bed time, pick them barbies up and brush your teeth so yall can get ready for bed" she said as we continued playing. Tish hated having to put her barbies away she would sit and play all day if she could. Which most days she did anyway. We took our barbie house's apart as we picked up to get ready for bed. We brushed our teeth, said goodnight to our mom and went into our rooms. As I get in my bed and turn off the light the silence gets loud. I switch positions trying to get comfortable so I can get fall asleep. I lay there looking at the ceiling my mind still racing. *Will this ever stop, will I ever not think so much?* I thought to myself as I lay there not knowing exactly what I expected to be on my mind. Before I know it the silence is way to loud, so I get up and go over to Tisha's room. "Can I lay with you" I said opening her door just barely knocking. She nods her head as she scoots over. Happy I didn't have to lay alone I run over and jump right in her bed. "Uh uh, you blocking my fan" she said pushing me because I was to high up. I start laughing as I scoot down. "Stop all that playing and go to bed" my mom yells from her room. We laugh a little more as we get comfortable. Tish was a thumb sucker to (snored some nights as well but I wont mention that again). She got under her cover, put her thumb in her mouth, and before I knew it she as sound asleep. I lay there on my side wondering how it was so easy for her to fall asleep. Maybe if I sucked my thumb to I giggled to myself. I lay still trying to not think to much. I knew if I started one thought more would come and they wouldn't stop. I close my eyes in the hopes of sleep coming easily. I fall asleep to my surprise with ease. As I sleep comfortably it only last a couple of hours. I jump out my sleep, feeling something touch my leg. Contrary to what I thought I was just Tish moving around in her sleep and our legs must have rubber each other. Breathing heavily and scared someone was there, I sit up and wipe my face. I look all around the room as my mind adjust with my eyes "Your at home pooh your ok" I say to myself. I lay back down, heart pounding but trying to calm my nerves down at the same time. As I lay there trying to go back to sleep I just cant. My heart wouldn't slow down and I just didn't see sleep happening after that moment. "I might as well go pee" I say to myself as I cant think of anything else to do. The house is quiet besides the sound of the fans going in the rooms. I walk softly and quietly to the bathroom trying not to wake anyone up. I walk in the bathroom still trying to collect my thoughts and understand I'm safe. I sit down and use the bathroom as I look around. Pulling myself together I notice my moms razor once again. I'm hesitant but I reach and pick it up anyway. Looking it over yet again my mind wonders if I can actually break it apart. I wipe myself and flush the toilet while still looking at the razor. I put it down on the sink and just stare at it. *"That thing is small that cant cut nothing"* I thought to myself. Trying to talk myself out of it, I turn to walk out the bathroom but my thoughts win. I turn back around make sure the door is locked and I do everything I can to break the razor open. Pulling at it, twisting and turning it so the plastic bends. Not to loud though I wouldn't dare want anyone to wake up and find out what I'm doing. Finally with out even realizing it, it breaks open and out falls three blades. I pick up each blade and just look at them in disbelief. *Do you really want to do this . Are you really about to do this?* With out even answering my own questions I swipe the blade across my arm as fast as I could. Blood instantly starts to surface and I feel my arm stinging. "Ouch" I say softly. Watching the blood fall off my arm onto the sink I feel relieved. "wow that wasn't that bad" I say as I'm getting more and more interested as the blood just falls and falls. I then realize I still have the blade in my hand

and swipe my arm again and before I knew it, it was again and again and again, swipe after swipe. Watching my arm slightly open and the blood just come out quicker and quicker I felt good. I felt a little bit of peace and anger all in one. I felt like I was letting poison out of my body. I was clearing out everything that was stuck inside of me that I couldn't find a way to get out. I finally figured out a way to let it out, it was all coming out and I could finally be free. As I sat in the bathroom pressing tissue on my arm to stop the bleeding I looked up and noticed my reflection. A slight smile came across my face. "You did it" I nodded to myself as I felt joy, pleasure, peace. I pressed onto my arm until the blood stopped flowing and I could only see the slashes on my arm. I sat in amazement just looing at them all over my arm. Looking at my release felt good it felt great even. I pull my sleeve down turn off the light and come out of the bathroom. I head over to my own room instead of Tisha's. I get in my bed still holding my arm laying down on my back. I smile to myself happily, relieved, feeling good. I close my eyes and fall to sleep happy for the first time in a very long time. When my mom comes in to wake me up the next day for school, it was almost like a dream. I feel my arm stinging, slightly sensitive to touch as I get up and head to the bathroom to brush my teeth. I make sure to spend enough time getting up that I don’t have to share the bathroom with Tish that morning. I hear her go in and get her self together as I wait for her to finish. She comes out the bathroom and I quickly walk in the bathroom I had to see what my arm looked like now .

CHAPTER 9

The weeks seemed to go by quicker, the weekend comes and goes quicker, and I continue to go to my aunt's house. Not too much happens though just like before. Abuse me, violate me, and just leave me alone until you need a fix. My mental battles became less and less. I eventually let the cutting take away any battle I was dealing with. One day when I was at school, I raised my hand to go to the restroom. Ms. Wisdom stopped for a second and just stared at me. “What” I said confused. “Nothing Calesha, what do you need” she replied kind of hesitant. “May I go to the bathroom please” I said smiling. Ms. Wisdom wasn’t like most adults, she was cool. Always made sure we had fun in her class and just kept us all laughing. I quickly got up, got the hall pass and went to the restroom. I didn’t really pay attention to the time but when I made it back everyone was out of the classroom and only Ms. Wisdom sat at her desk. “Oh, is it lunch time” I said shocked to see the classroom empty. “Calesha come have a seat please” she said so gently. Nervously I walk over to her desk and sit in the chair in front of her. “Do you want to talk about anything with me Calesha” her soft voice let out with tears in her eyes. “No” I said quietly as I pulled on my sleeves knowing she must know something. “I noticed some things on your arms you don’t want to talk about that” still talking softly. I put my head down to avoid eye contact with her. “If you ever feel like you want to talk about things that are hard to talk about, I am always willing to listen to you, no matter how bad no matter how tough” her sweet voice said. Ms. Wisdom was always telling jokes and laughing with us. To hear the hurt in her voice broke my heart, I wanted to hug her and just tell her everything but every ounce in me said NO don’t say a word. I continued to sit with my head down as she just stared at me pleading with her eyes for me to say something anything. But I couldn’t, I couldn’t face her. *Would she think I was disgusting; would she think I let this happen, how far back would I even go and talk about it?* After what seemed like forever of her staring at me, I finally got the courage to pick my head up. With the nicest smile I could force my face to make, I looked her right in her eyes and said “I'm ok I promise I get a little upset sometimes but I'm getting better” I lied. “Honey, I saw your arm, that doesn’t look like a little upset” she said placing her hand on her lap and turning her chair towards me. “Oh that, that’s old I don’t do that anymore that was a while ago that happened” I continued to lie. “Aww sweety” she said so concerned. “Ms. Wisdom I'm ok I promise, there was some things I needed to work through, but I don’t do that anymore” pointing quickly to my arm. “Can I go eat my lunch” I stood up talking. Her eyes were watery, and I felt so much empathy coming from her eyes. “Go ahead sweety” she said crossing her arms. I turn to walk out but before I get to the door “Calesha” she calls out. “You can always talk to me remember that ok sweetheart” I nod and walk out the door. The rest of the day I asked myself *why I didn’t tell her, why didn’t I just open up and tell her.* Little did I know this was the beginning of me being closed off and never talking to anyone about anything going on with me. Being 31 now I realize how hard it still is for me to open up to people. I can be “that person” for pretty much everyone in my life but I can never let anyone close enough to be “that person” to me. That day when I got home from school, I just knew Ms. Wisdom called my mom and I was about to have to explain when I got home. We lived right across the street from the school, so I walked as slowly as possible once the bell rang for us to go home. I walked as slow as I could to have my plans together and my story straight. How the hell am I going to explain this? *Maybe I can tell her it happened at school, and it was an accident with some scissors.* I thought as I held my arm. *Mom is not dumb this is not going to work!* I thought to myself. As I got closer to home, I took a deep breath as I walked up the front steps. My mom wasn’t home, the house was quiet. I ran to my room and closed the door. As I push my sleeve up, I see old scars, new scars, and just marks all over. “Shit” I thought as I looked at it, I didn’t know I did it that much I said to myself. I went to the bathroom and wet a warm rag. I wipe away some smudged blood, puss, and particles from my shirt stuck in the wounds, and put a good amount of ointment on it. I pull my sleeve down and look up to see I'm in the spot I hate the most. Right in front of the mirror. Yet again having to face myself. I shake my head as I'm forced to look at what I hate to see the most. “You're so stupid you can't even cut yourself and hide it right, now she gone call your mom and then what?” I asked myself. Upset I was caught and sure to get in trouble I just stared at myself until I began to cry. I sat on the floor in front of the sink and pulled my sleeve up. Slightly in pain, I see my arm shiny from the medicine and red from the pain. I just looked at it, rubbed it, and just cried. *“Wtf am I doing to myself”* I thought. Just as soon as the thought came out, I heard the front door close. “Pooh you home” I heard the voice yell. I jumped up, wiped my face, and pulled my sleeve down. “Coming” I yell trying to pull myself together. I take a deep breath as I prepare to open the bathroom door. I can hear the footsteps coming up the stairs and I prepare to face the voice. “Hey pooh” said Tish as she went past me to go into her room. Without even realizing I'm holding my breath, I release it. “Whew” I say relieved it wasn’t my mom. “How was school” she said from her room as I walked past her going into my room. “It was ok” I lie as I close my door. I fall asleep as I lay in my bed stuck in my normal spot, MY THOUGHTS.

I can't lie, my life was pretty much a downward spiral at that point. I didn't really care much for my friends. I became more and more distant with my family and just felt so misunderstood. I still don’t know why Ms. Wisdom didn’t call my mom. Some might say she failed me and should have reported it, some might understand the bond and the amount of trust we had for each other, and just assume she trusted my word that I didn’t do it anymore. I honestly can't tell you. I continued to go hang out with my cousin, not too much happened there anymore, I later in life was thankful for this. We got older, Megan and I got different interests, and it just wasn’t the same going over with her. I mean she was a couple years older than me. I was in Jr high she was in high school; she didn’t have time to really be bothered with me. Growing up we moved ALOT. Always a different school, always a new room. I just went with the flow most of my life. Once my arms were noticed by Ms. Wisdom, I really stopped cutting, it wasn't for a long time though. It eventually came back around but that's at another point in my life. I started finding more cousins to hang out with and it was like my nightmare never really ended. No matter where I went it was always a different devil just waiting to attack. I didn't care though I knew I could go to happier places in my mind and just come back when it was over. Cutting was still a release once things started back up in different places with different people. Only as time went on, I got older, and I got smarter. I would cut things that weren't shown, like my thighs my stomach. Places that only I could see. Well besides the ones who invaded those areas, but do you think they ever noticed? Nope and if they did, they never mentioned it. But then again how would they explain seeing that!

CHAPTER 10

Things got dark for me for a very long time. I honestly didn't focus on the bad anymore, I just kind of let things happen and became immune. We moved often, my mom got married, she had another child. Thats my little sister Ariauna. Life just pretty much went on, the abuse never stopped. I was never safe, and I pretty much gave up on the thought of ever being safe. One night I was between 12 and 14. I remember my mom doing my hair. Me, her and my sister Tish sat in my room as she focused on what style to give us. It was pretty quiet, and I really can't even tell you how the conversation started. But I remember asking my mom what she would do if someone was doing things to us that they weren't supposed to. I won't make it out to be a big issue I'm healing and I'm getting over it but basically, she didn't have much to say. "Things like that just kind of happens in black homes." That was all I needed to hear before I didn't need to hear anymore. I got older, and I got rebellious. Fighting all the time, skipping school. I eventually turned to marijuana to ease the pain. It felt good cutting got old, it wasn't making me feel as good as it used to. I eventually created this "box" in my mind. I vowed to put every horrible thing stuck my mind in there, and chain it closed. There was no reason to let it have a hold on my life anymore, no reason to think about it. I was in my teen years, and I was so busy being a busy teenager no one had time to even have access to me anymore. It's sad and it's a messed-up way to feel but hey whatever works, works. I avoided sleeping, I avoided basements, I avoided talking about my life, and I avoided men. I understand that only two people were explained in this book but that was my most traumatic experiences. The ones that still haunt me, the ones that keep me up at night, and make sure I never forget their face, forget their touch, forget the hold they have on me. All the family after that hurt me, abused me really didn't matter. I was used by then, I was use to the feeling, use to the way things happened and numb to it all. Nothing could be done to me worse than what had already been done. My innocence was gone at such a young age. My mind no longer capable of processing. I was forced to grow up before I was even able to be a kid. The stigma that surrounds sex abuse and molestation is baffling to me. Now that I'm a mom, and my daughter is growing and growing every day I am terrified for her. Her body is filling out, her features are becoming more noticeable, and my heart breaks every time I see the changes in her. The way grown men view children these days is sickening. It always has been, and it needs to be talked about more, children need to know the signs. They need to know about unsafe touches, and they need to know when it feels wrong, that's because it is! There is no such thing as secrets, tell mom or dad, we are your secret keepers, in case you forget telling us will help, we can hold all the secrets for you! I am now a mom of 3 beautiful kids, and I worry every day about each of them, not just my daughter, but my sons as well. Break the stigma of it just happening in families, and it being "normal", break the stigma of it only happening to little girls as well. Boys go through it just like little girls. My stories are just a few of many that people still go through every day. It's time to break those generational curses, talk to your kids. Be their safe space, be their voice when they feel they don't have one. Kids talk to their parents as well. It is ok, I know I wasn't believed when I finally did speak up but speak up until someone believes you! Someone WILL believe you. Don't let your voice be silenced. My voice was silenced for 25 years. But no more, I will no longer be quiet. It's time to let go of that hurt, get rid of that pain. I tried my best to find any outlet that I could to ease the pain and quiet the thoughts, but nothing ever fully worked. Here I am now, still trying to cope, trying to ***UNDERSTAND***. I don't go into basements, it's hard to be sexually active and like it. I barely sleep, and when I do, I'm a very light sleeper, I don't sleep long, and I don't sleep hard. I don't trust people and I can't handle simple compliments. All my life I was told how "pretty" I was but look what being so pretty got me. My biggest point is don't let things in your life define you or define your life. Wake up every day and FIGHT. Fight for you, fight for your voice, and fight for your future self. To all the young ladies and grown woman who go through these things past present or future, I just want you to know you are not alone. I hear you; I see you, and I'm here to be your voice until you can be your own. I'm ready to fight the fight! "Hey pretty" will forever be a hard thing for me to hear, but "Hey pretty" changed my life. I'm finally understanding this thing called life a little more. Understand what happened to you, and work through those built-up emotions and feelings. You are beautiful, you are loved, and you are worth it! Life will always throw us curve balls and no one ever deserves to go through these type of things and my heart truly goes out to people who have had it worse than what I did. Rather that be molested, sexual abuse, rape, any of the sort, it does get better once you work through it. Its not easy, its far from easy but trust that God has your back and will get you through it. I know there's some people who will question, *"how can God allow something like this to happen"?* That is all apart of the understanding! You see we come back time after time, generation after generation and sometimes we are chosen to break that curse. I'm sure there was plenty family members before me that went through these type of things as well but who spoke up to stop it?! Thats what breaking generational curses are all about! I'm breaking generational curses for my KIDS, for my future grandkids and great grandkids and so on and so forth. You don't understand how much power is behind simply speaking up and being heard. NO MORE, not in my legacy! Generations to come after me will have a voice because I am bringing that change into fruition! Improper touches, molestation, sex abuse, that soul contract is closed for my future family. I'm now planting fresh seeds and growing fresh roots. I understand why thins happened how they di now that I've improved my relationship with God. I was chosen, hand picked to put a stop to the chaos that my family and so many other families endured for so many generations! God gives his toughest battles to his strongest soldiers, I'm stepping up in ways that have never been done for my family and I am humbled, I am blessed and I UNDERSTAND! My life's motto is understand, accept and release. You've now taken a walk down my journey of understanding. Hopefully I will see you in my next chapter of accepting! We never stop learning we never stop growing and never stop releasing. I’m going through my accept part of my life and things aren’t easy but I’m making it work. With the help of God, my spirit team, and my ancestors, we are all making it!

"UNDERSTAND, ACCEPT, RELEASE"

Many blessings, keep fighting, keep pushing, be heard!

Made in the USA
Columbia, SC
14 February 2024

9e191ce7-7711-43ba-86ad-232340d1a7a5R01